RANDY HANNAH & DONALD ROSE

# When Life Hands You Lemons, You Hand Them Back!

*When Life Hands You Lemons*

First published by The Write Brothers 2019

Copyright © 2019 by Randy Hannah & Donald Rose

All rights reserved. No part of this publication may be reproduced, stored or transmitted in any form or by any means, electronic, mechanical, photocopying, recording, scanning, or otherwise without written permission from the publisher. It is illegal to copy this book, post it to a website, or distribute it by any other means without permission.

Randy Hannah & Donald Rose asserts the moral right to be identified as the author of this work.

Randy Hannah & Donald Rose has no responsibility for the persistence or accuracy of URLs for external or third-party Internet Websites referred to in this publication and does not guarantee that any content on such Websites is, or will remain, accurate or appropriate.

Designations used by companies to distinguish their products are often claimed as trademarks. All brand names and product names used in this book and on its cover are trade names, service marks, trademarks and registered trademarks of their respective owners. The publishers and the book are not associated with any product or vendor mentioned in this book. None of the companies referenced within the book have endorsed the book.

First edition

ISBN: 978-0-692-19068-5

This book was professionally typeset on Reedsy.
Find out more at reedsy.com

Remember that champions are like grass whose natural tendency is to grow and flourish. Like the grass, cut me down as you may and I will rise and flourish again.

       The Write Brothers

# Contents

| | |
|---|---|
| *Acknowledgement* | ii |
| Introduction | 1 |
| Unshackled | 3 |
| Good Times | 9 |
| Silver Spoons | 14 |
| The Jefferson's | 20 |
| Champions | 26 |
| Summary | 32 |
| About the Authors | 38 |

# Acknowledgement

We must pay homage and respect to our brothers, sisters, and great mentors. Those who have come before us to light the path as we continue to keep the path lit. Napoleon Hill, Neville Goddard, Bob Proctor, Zig Ziglar, Kevin Trudeau, Rhonda Byrne, Maxwell Maltz, Andrew Carnegie, Abraham Hicks, Deepak Chopra, and Earl Nightingale just to name a few.

Without these people and their desire to reveal to the world the power of the human mind and the power of human thought, without their desire to simplify the law of attraction and make it known to us that our connection to god is that we are god, without this information we believe that an entire world would be lost. We are ever grateful to the beautiful creation that we experience every day. The splendor of the rising sun peeking through the beautiful cloud cover, and the awesome display of autumn colors as the leaves change out for winter, we see a beautiful array of colors, orange, red, yellow, and green all bristling vibrantly as the sun sets and plays peak-a-boo through the trees.

These great wonders are a reflection of the mind of the one we call source energy, or god, or the creator, and we are awestruck that this creation was made for us to admire, and designed to inspire us and so we are inspired to bring acknowledgement to those who truly delivered this message, through us as a channel. We have done nothing more than continued the message, like a reporter just reporting the facts, because we do not have the last say on the matter, there are many who came before us, those who are now awake and those who will wake up in the near future to the message of hope and deliverance provided when we take control of our mind and possess it!

# 1

# Introduction

Many people believe the saying when life hands you lemons you make lemonade. This is a big fat WRONG! We want to let you know that this mindset is for suckers, for people who do not want to fight for what belongs to them. They are okay with not getting what they want out of life. They gossip about what Mr. Jones has, but are frowning from the tangy taste of the lemonade they've made. All the while, Mr. Jones sips on his Mango tea. This group accepts whatever life gives them. They are afraid to rock the boat so they go along with the status quo even though they hate it. For instance, the person, who constantly is passed over for promotions and raises, instead of them asking why they were not considered or simply looking for work elsewhere, they just work harder for the next promotion.

In the bible, the book of Luke, chapter 18 verses 1-8, speaks of a widow in a certain city who came to the Judge and pleaded for justice against her adversary, and the Judge refused. Moreover, the woman refused. She refused to accept the Judge's ruling against her, so she came back continually and for a time he refused her request continually. The Judge grew weary of her continual requests. He grew tired of her consistency and persistence. The Judge was so whipped by her continual coming that he awarded her the request just so she would stop coming. We have to keep coming at life in this manner, refusing to accept less than what we are worth, daring to ask for more with boldness. When life hands you lemons you hand them back! This means that you must become resolute about what you want and expect from life. Therefore, when you are determined to get something accomplished and something or someone gets in your way, from now on you"ll know that you do not have to take it. You do not have to make lemonade. You do not have to accept the conditions of life that you are currently in as the finale.

So just how do you give the lemons back? We are glad you were wondering about that because that is what this book is all about. We want to begin helping you give those lemons back by helping you understand why you think you have to make lemonade in the first place. Now before we get into this we must make a few disclaimers. The bible is referenced in this book as a literary work only and our reference to it does not endorse any religious ideology. Secondly, if you like getting lemons then make your lemonade and enjoy it. For those who like mangoes, apples, oranges, peaches, and the sweeter things in life, this is for you.

# 2

# Unshackled

If you were born into wealth or as some like to put it, born with a Silver Spoon in your mouth, then you have never needed to adopt the mindset that comes from lack of money and resources. Making lemonade out of lemons is a philosophy for poor people (those who lack financial resources and those with a poor mindset). What we mean is that most poor people's view or state of mind, is that of always (being) poor or not having enough, this conditions their beliefs about themselves and fixes their state of being poor, or always knowing of themselves as poor. Sadly, the majority believe they are powerless over what happens to them in life and simply conform and make the best out of the little they have. Viewing yourself as poor, or unworthy even though you do not have the money you desire, is what we call having a poor self-image and we will touch on this in a later chapter. Beyoncé created an entire movement behind this philosophy with her Lemonade Album and videos explaining the thought behind the whole idea. Her concept is based on her and her husbands' grandmothers' belief system. According to a Wikipedia entry, "The album title was inspired by Beyoncé's grandmother Agnéz Deréon, as well as her husband Jay-Z's grandmother, Hattie White. At the end of the track "Freedom", an audio recording of Hattie White speaking to a crowd at her 90th birthday party in December 2015 is played. During the speech, Hattie says, "I had my ups and downs, but I always find the inner strength to pull myself up. I was served lemons, but I made lemonade". That means she was given something in life that she did not necessarily want, but she found a way to deal with it and make it work. We suppose that making it work is fine, but what if she really wanted more? Beyoncé and we are all from Houston Texas and pretty close in age. We do not know her, her husband, or their grandmothers, but we can guarantee you that their grandmothers and our grandmothers had a whole lot in common. Their philosophy on life was most certainly passed down to us in some way, shape, form, or fashion.

Many of our ancestors had a way of thinking about life. They believed that if they just kept praying, singing, and struggling, God would eventually hear their cries and provide some miracle that would change their circumstances. They thought that because they were poor financially and despised socially that this was somehow a test of their faith in God and their lot in life. They believed that they could only do their best in their present state. Many pastors and religious teachers reinforced this belief every single Sunday, or if you grew up as we did, every Saturday at Church. They would remind us that suffering is a trait of Christianity or a symbol of your connection to God. Man, please stop it! Suffering, poverty, and lack, contrary to popular belief, are not traits of holiness or evidence of your humility and faith in God. They are traits of brokenness and evidence that something is off in your thought process.

There is a charge from God, which says be ye Holy for I am Holy.

However, what does it actually mean to be Holy? To be Holy means to be separate and distinct from that which is common or ordinary. Just look it up in the Hebrew. It is the word qadosh. Jesus once said, "I came that YOU might have life, and that more abundantly". So which one is it? Do you accept the struggle, poverty, and poor man's mindset of lack? On the other hand, do you accept the mind of Christ, which is abundance? The common ordinary mindset is that of lack, scarcity, and making lemonade out of lemons. Just look around you the examples are endless of people accepting life as is. They make no effort whatsoever to improve themselves. The only work experience they've ever had is as a fast food worker or customer service rep, and if this is you my friend, then you are in need of some new skills and perhaps more education, otherwise, you will keep getting lemons.

However, if your desire in life is to work at Burger King or Wal-Mart and work your way up in their matrix, then you my friend are living your dream. You have gotten what you desired from life. To those who feel that they want more let us warn you that giving lemons back is not an easy feat. It is going to take some real consistent work but that is what makes it holy. It is not common or ordinary for people to refuse what appears to be their lot in life. The Holy mind, the separate and distinct mind, is that of abundance. The mindset that says I am not leaving until I get what I came for is holy. Being holy is, knowing that all things truly are possible to those that believe. It is the mind that knows, without doubt, that you can make life yield to you that which you really want. It all comes down to what you currently believe about yourself and what you are willing to bring yourself to believe. That is one of the keys, the BRINGING of you to believe. This giving lemons back business is not for the timid or cowardly.

This is going against all that your mother and father taught you and all that your pastor taught you. This is going to challenge many religious teachings and traditions that you may hold near and dear, but those teachings, those traditions are holding you hostage. There is an entire country of people who were enslaved for a great number of years and endured heinous acts of violence and treachery. For illustrative purposes, let us call them Africans. We know the American version of the history of these people and if history is our teacher, then what did we learn from people like Nat Turner, Fredrick Douglass, Madam CJ Walker, Harriet Tubman, Dr. Martin Luther King Jr., and Malcolm X? The list goes on and on about people who refused to accept their circumstances as final, even though the law was written against them, and their desires for freedom. Did they roll over and just take it? Did they just make lemonade? Hell to the no!

They took their freedom by any means necessary even if it meant they would die, at least they would be free in death. Or what about this other Country we know of today as America, when they were taxed to the toenail by the Crown of England? Did Americans make lemonade? No! They gave those lemons back and a fight came with it. An entire war was waged behind the matter.

We are not advocating violence or suggesting extremism toward people, but we are saying that you must become violent against your own mindset of old thought patterns if you are going to hand lemons back.

You must be willing to eradicate a belief system which, number one, is not your own, and number two, does not serve your desires. You must be willing to become extreme in your desire to rise above a position in life that you do not like being in. You must push back when you get pushed by life. Push back in the same manner with which those who came before us did when life seemingly denied them. The main barriers we face often are our present beliefs. The problem about these beliefs is that they were programmed in us during our youth, when we could not think for ourselves. By the time we were able to think for ourselves, we were so deeply indoctrinated, that any thought contrary to the thoughts we were given were deemed blasphemy.

When you begin thinking for yourself, you will discover that things are much different from what you have been taught. You'll experience, for the first time perhaps, what it feels like to actively use your brain. You'll know what it feels like to be in the command center, sitting at the control board, directing your own life. When you begin asking yourself the question, why you believe what you believe, you will start to see that you really don't believe much of what you thought you did. You will see that your current belief's, fears, doubts, attitudes and the like, all came from somebody else. Parents, teachers, and some pastors meant well passing down ideals and traditions to their captive audiences. However, certain traditions passed from one generation to the next are a collective effort to steer people down a path that has been tested and proven to keep you on the hamster wheel of life. The problem with this is that the tradition took no account for evolution and more importantly, it took no account of people waking up to the fact that you can create your own tradition. The old saying "If it was good enough for granny it's good enough for me" just doesn't cut it anymore.

In all fairness, they could only teach what they were taught. Sadly, the same program is being implemented in public schools and churches right now. Believe me, teaching people how to think critically and independently is not high on the priority list of the education department. In most church settings, thinking for yourself is not an option either, you are told not to question god or that your mind is finite, and cannot comprehend the infinite things of god. You will soon discover too, that some of your own family and close friends will no longer want to associate with you because you now think and believe differently from them. So you can now begin to see why you think you have to accept lemons, and why you think you have to make lemonade.

Who taught you that stuff? Well it does not matter now because you are responsible for what you think and how you think. Ultimately, you are responsible for your circumstances. So, does this mean we are handing ourselves lemons? More on that later in chapter 5, but you have to stop letting other people tell you how to think and start thinking for yourself. True freedom is in thinking for yourself and drawing your own conclusions about what you experience in life.

So if you hold on to this poverty and lack mindset, you are most certainly guaranteed to get exactly what you deserve from life. Life only yields to those who are fearless, bold, and most importantly it only yields to those who know what they want and refuse to accept less than what they've asked for.

## 3

# Good Times

As youngsters, there was a particular television show that we would watch regularly. The name of the show was Good Times. Good Times aired in 1974 and it captured the life of a family living below the poverty line in an impoverished neighborhood in the USA. The setting was the infamous Cabrini Green Apartments on the north side of Chicago Illinois. The family was always struggling and didn't have enough money. Food was scarce at times too, and the Cabrini Green projects was overrun with criminal activity. The story line was about the family constantly scratching and surviving. James Evans, who was the Father on the show was a no nonsense type of dad. His character was very stern but his attitude was applied in error. His attitude should have been no nonsense when it came down to his living conditions.

The television show also gave us a snapshot of a particular mindset. People who believe that they can't do better will continue to keep their family living in dangerous conditions. For example, when you listen to the show's theme song, it's quite disturbing how the song encourages making the best life with the little bit you have, it actually say's ain't we lucky, wow! It may have been a song about the way life was during that era but that's the problem. The show and theme song reinforced a way of living that did not have to be. Now don't get us wrong, We understand when people are born into or fall on hard times they need certain platforms to get them on their feet. But the bottom line is that, your mindset catapults you from where you are to where you want to be, or holds you back.

The theme song for Good Times was quite catchy. It's easy to find yourself just humming along to the melody, But, as we got older, the lyrics to the theme song had us scratching our heads in disbelief. The song promotes the central theme that no matter how bad it gets, it's okay to settle for less because you're going to make it through somehow, so just make a "good time" with whatever you have. Now in some regard, we get what they were trying to say, but that philosophy will trap you in a vicious cycle of accepting lemons when that's not what you really want. The scratching and surviving mentality, keeping your head above water, are yellow ripe lemons that must be handed back immediately.

The television show "Good Times", also seemed to highlight the shortcomings of the family. Every time they seemed to get a break, something would always happen to stifle the progress they'd made, and pulled them right back down. We must recondition the mind or be doomed forever into making lemonade out of lemons. Having good times does not consist of scraping to get by, living for the weekend, or staying on welfare forever.

We used to exhibit this behavior until we were enlightened with the truth that we've been lied to by those who didn't know the truth themselves. However, there is no more blaming anyone or anything for the mindset of accepting the sub-par and making the best out of the scraps of life. No more believing that when something bad happens to you, you're stuck with the drudgery, with no way to make it out. That is far, far away from the truth and damn sure not the definition of "Good Times".

"I remember the first time I heard music. I literally fell in love with the poetry, melodies, and compositions of songs. I loved it so much, that I overloaded my brain trying to figure out how I could make recordings of myself. Even though I didn't have any music equipment or the money to pay for studio time, I knew there had to be an alternative. So I would imagine myself day and night recording songs and producing records. When I told others about my aspirations, they immediately started handing me lemons. Every response from people I knew, young and old was contrary to my beliefs. Just imagine how many future doctors, lawyers, dancers, comedians, and activist's dreams are crushed daily from listening to and believing the "Good Times" mentality of someone else.

Despite their attempts to serve me with a dish of sour lemons, I refused to listen and my desire to do music increased. One day I got an idea in my bedroom. I had a radio with a dual cassette and a microphone jack. I plugged my headphones into the mic jack, pressed record, and made my first clean sounding demo. That's another story in itself but the point is that I had such a longing to accomplish this goal; I searched and searched and searched until my imagination pushed me to figure out how to do it. I refused to accept lemons. I refused to believe that I needed a recording studio to record my ideas. As I continued I got the chance to record in a real studio. My mastery of writing, and recording sessions got better, my skills increased, and I began to create a buzz. I was able to headline concerts and signed an independent record deal. Oh, I also have my own recording studio at my house now. I like to think of this time as receiving my mango-blueberry medley. And to think it all started with me handing the lemons back which led to me receiving what I really wanted."

The bottom line here is that it's all a choice but you have to make the choice or the choice will be made for you. Do you sink or swim, you choose. Do you fight or get rolled over, that's your call. Do you make the lemonade or hand those lemons back? For the sake of this book, you hand those lemons back. We're highlighting the theme song of this show because it has lead us to believe that there were no other options other than to just roll over and accept the humble pie of lack. Fuck keeping our heads above water, we're getting out of the water to find a boat so we can ride it out the rest of the way, and we'd suggest you do the same. If you want to be humble and beggarly then go to church. You weren't placed on this earth to watch asphalt grow, you came here to live the great life of I Am, I can have, and I can do. Prosperity has never been overrated and it never will be. The question is will you bring yourself to believe that you can use your imagination to change your own life?

So what do good times actually look like? What does it feel like? What does it smell like? What does it taste like? Good times begin with forgetting everything you've ever been taught about making lemonade out of lemons. Good times begin with a positive mindset, the kind of mind that says I can do it. Good times are more than keeping your head above water it's using your mind to rise up out of the water. A good time comes with making better choices to create a great legacy for you and your family. Whether it's putting your money together to invest, launching a crowd-funding project with two or three friends you trust, or believing in yourself and your dreams when nobody else does. All in all, you have to believe that you have the right to hand those lemons back. If you don't want lemons, you sure as hell shouldn't take them. Set goals for yourself, believe in yourself and your goals, visualize the end result, and use those dreams as seeds and let the Good Times roll!

# 4

# Silver Spoons

Do you remember the hit television show Silver Spoons that first aired in 1982? Well if you don't you should research it on YouTube. The pilot episode was about a very rich guy named Edward Stratton III and his estranged son Ricky Stratton. Edward, the father had every material possession a kid could want, ping pong table, arcade games, Pinball machines, a real life size train and track running through the house. He didn't just have grown up toys, he had a house designed for a kid to have a fantasy all their own and he didn't even know he had a child. One day this little boy shows up to his house, rings the doorbell and says tah dah I'm your son. The kid is amazed at how many toys his adult father has. As the story goes, it appeared that the rich guy did not care much about the day-to-day transactions of life; he focused on having a good time in the moment. He was so caught up in feeling good and having fun that when his business manager and his lawyer told him he was broke, he simply said, "I can't be broke! I WAS BORN RICH AND I WILL DIE RICH". He told them, the problem was that they lacked faith, and they would figure out what was going on. After all was said and done, he went right back to playing video games.

Now his business partner and lawyer were looking at his bank account and they knew there was no more money. Despite the fact that he was just hit with the bombshell of having a son he did not know about, this guy refused to give any attention to the thought that he was broke. He rejected the lemons that life handed him in that moment. He spoke of only the life he was used to and only saw himself as rich even though he had actually gone broke. Now we want to take you back to chapter three Good Times. This family was born with a wooden spoon in their mouths. They saw themselves as poor and lacking. Their mindset had them view themselves as people who were destined to struggle through life, scratching and surviving. They had only a dim hope of ever getting enough money to live the good life.

Our point here is to draw the contrast between the two types of mindsets. We also want to compare the thought process of these two groups. In one hand, we have a guy who was born with a silver spoon in his mouth and when told that he was in the same financial position as the characters from Good Times, he rejected the thought. Better yet in that moment, he handed those lemons back. In the other hand, the people from Good Times accepted the lemons and made lemonade. We know that for the duration of the show Good Times, all they ever got were lemons. They finally made it out of the ghetto but that was only because it was the last episode of the show and the writers wanted to end on a positive note. Now the father in Silver Spoons ended up finding his money, well actually Edward Stratton's son Ricky found the money. Yep ole Ricky eavesdropped on a conversation that his father's business manager was having and he discovered that the business manager had ripped his father off. Talk about life handing you lemons. Nonetheless, they continued on living the good life.

Many people think in terms of where they are in the present moment, instead we must think in terms of where we want to be. If you are used to not having much and used to things not working in your favor, then believe me when it comes to being successful or having thoughts of success, you will remind yourself, that you have never had anything, by doing something stupid to destroy your own opportunities. We refer to this as self-sabotage because of poor self-image. Self-image is that picture of ourselves that we have on the inside. When you get something good going and your state of being is that of poverty, when the outside picture doesn't match the inside picture, you do something to cause the outside picture, to match the inside picture that you have of yourself, at which point you can now say, "see I told you nothing ever goes my way". Again, here we are saying that you have total power over everything that goes on in your life, you just have to be consciously aware of how you are thinking, and you will be able to sense the ability to arrest a bad thought and put it to death. We can hear you saying it's easy to think thoughts of abundance when you have abundance, but let us remind you of this fact: you've had abundance all of your life and you just didn't know it. There is no such thing as not enough, there is only abundance. Look, around you, we have never run out of anything. The world around us is showing us daily that there is only abundance. If there were a such thing as lack then, when a single apple seed is planted it would only give us, a tree with one apple and one seed in it. We all know that we get multiple apples and those apples have multiple seeds in them, do you care to know why? It's because there is only abundance, there is no such thing as not enough.

Well why is it that some people have it all and others seem to be lacking? Lack is a condition of how we think about ourselves, and more importantly, lack is a condition we accept. Instead of thinking from the position of there is only abundance, instead of looking through the glasses of where we want to be, we focus only on what we see in front of us. Instead, we should be thinking about that apple which proved to us that there is only abundance. The guy from Silver Spoons understood the principle of abundance and the family from Good Times did not. They only focused on the no can do part of life, they never focused on the can do part. The truth is that, even though they were not born with a Silver Spoon, they could most certainly get the capital to buy one.

If you are living in conditions that you don't like, what will you do to change it? Handing lemons back will require you to do more than you are used to doing, it is going to require you to believe in yourself and your dreams when nobody else does. It is going to require you to fight back and stand your ground. Maybe your family has always been poor and you did not have a rich uncle who died and left you a fortune, so what! Have you ever thought that it's your responsibility to build the family legacy of wealth? Has it ever dawned on you that you are the chosen one to start a family business, that you are to become that rich uncle or auntie who sets the financial tone for the future of your family? Stop hating on the Silver Spooner's and start adopting their way of thinking. They know without question that there is only abundance and they know that having abundance feels good. This is another key to handing lemons back, knowing that there is only abundance, and feeling good about it.

That is why the Silver Spoons character only focused on having fun, and feeling good, he knew there is only abundance and he did things that reminded him of that fact. Contrary to popular belief, you are always supposed to feel good and have fun. The bible states in the book of Ecclesiastes that there is nothing better for man; his lot in life is to eat, drink, and be merry. This sounds like we are supposed to have fun and feel good all the time. But because we have been conditioned by religion and propaganda to believe that it's somehow more honorable to suffer, we take the lemons and make lemonade.

When are you going to throw away this belief system? You suffer in silence praying for deliverance all while you watch other people go after what they want and they get it. They may be praying too, but the difference is that after they finish praying they do not wait on the lord, they understand that the lord is within them already and they go after it and get it, whatever IT is. They know and understand what faith without works means. You have to become selfish. Yes, I said be selfish. There is nothing wrong with being selfish. Selfish people get ahead in life. Being self-serving and self-centered is often confused with selfishness. To be selfish is to be focused on what you want and refusing to allow anyone or anything to stop you from accomplishing your goals. It is saying to friends and family I can't hang out this month I have to focus on some things.

Selfishness is sacrifice. It is saying NO when you want to say yes. Being self-centered and self-serving are completely about other people serving you. It is about you doing things so that the results benefit you, regardless of what happens to someone else. Selfishness says, that what I am seeking to accomplish will benefit other people. If I am not whole, how can I help someone else be whole? Being self-centered says that I am whole, and you had better figure out how to become whole. The only way we can be of help to others is if we first take care of self. Self-preservation is the first rule of law and nature. Therefore, it is natural to secure self, first. If god is in man, then man is god or god like, and putting self-first is putting god first in everything you do.

So if you're living in circumstances or conditions that you know, you don't really want to be in, then get selfish, make some sacrifices and secure the life you really want. Start handing those lemons back now!

# 5

# The Jefferson's

George Jefferson. This man is one of the first television characters that we could remember, who took no crap from anybody and lived by his own rules, as you may recall from his role on the hit television show All in the Family in the early 1970's. The Jefferson's, which aired in 1975, was a spin off from All In The Family where George's wife, Louise Jefferson, was a "Colored" maid for Archie Bunker and his family. This is what made the Jefferson's such a significant show. On the set of the Jefferson's, George was a firm family man, and a genuine friend, he was brutally honest with his opinions and most importantly, he took no lemons, and his wife Louise now enjoyed having her own maid. He acquired his success through hard work and perseverance. During times of inequality, he developed a "don't quit" mentality. Under no circumstances would he allow anyone to give him lemonade when he wanted scotch in a highball glass. George Jefferson represented a way of thinking that to some would seem cocky and arrogant, but when you come up from the bottom, you will go all out to make sure you never return to that place of despair, unless you come back to share knowledge as a gift, real jewels for the people.

This "unwavering" mentality should be the prototype for us all who have dreams and visions of being successful in whatever field we have a burning desire to conquer. You have heard the stories of those who almost crossed the finish line, and got distracted by doubt, fear, and the opinions of others. These distractions are mainly coming from your thoughts and should be subdued with aggressive mental opposition. What we mean is that you have the power to switch your thoughts in the middle of what we call a thought transaction. When you know the thought is inaccurate, immediately stop that flow of energy by switching your thought to that which makes you happy, or makes you feel good.

For example, if you were listening to country music on 99.1 FM and then you wanted to hear some jazz, what would you do? You would change the station to one that is playing the music that you want to hear. You do not keep on listening to what you do not like, even if you choose to play some mp3's or internet radio streaming. You would simply change the station. The point is that you are in control of your thoughts all of the time. You control your thoughts and feelings. Other people can perhaps influence you but you still make the final decision. For many years, we have allowed our minds and imaginations to run on autopilot, and they run wild.

This grabbing a hold of the reigns of your own mind and imagination is slippery at first, like trying to hold on to a fish fresh out of water. Nevertheless, with a little patience and practice, you will soon be in full command of your thoughts and imagination. Your confidence is at its greatest when you use your power of choice and choose to believe in yourself, especially when faced with a task where it would seem you have no chance to succeed. The main reason many people fail to conquer their world and guide their own ship to safe harbor, is self-doubt. We are the ones giving ourselves lemons most of the time. We ultimately decide how we feel. As soon as you wake up in the morning, the biggest decision you have to make before getting out of bed is what energy are you going to invest in for the rest of the day? What is going to be your attitude for the day?

It's kind of like getting dressed for the day, except you are getting your mind dressed for the day. You must go into the wardrobe of your mind and pick out the finest attitude to wear. If you do not have any fine attitude attire, then we suggest you obtain a brand new attitude. Our attitude determines whether we receive that big promotion, or receive a layoff notice. If it is one thing you should take away from this chapter it would be that "Our Energy or Attitude is everything". Our entire outlook, attitude, and energy right now will create the pathways and roads we will use to travel into our future.

The message of the Jefferson's theme song mixed with the bold aura and personality of George Jefferson is a rich recipe for success. Add to that mix, determination, strong conviction, and staying power, then you become who you want to be. Becoming a successful business owner and moving on up was a gigantic feat for a man who was raised by a family of sharecroppers. Just imagine the mental fortitude and endurance it required to succeed on that level during a time when there was no equality, a time when wealth was more of a priority than life itself. We must do just as George Jefferson did when he visualized his dream of becoming a business owner, before actually accomplishing one goal. He started at the end where the fish did not fry in the kitchen and beans did not burn on the grill. He saw himself, in his imagination, walking from room to room and he knew every square inch of his family's new luxury apartment in Manhattan, all while still residing in the working class section of Queens. By using the resources he was given at birth "his mind & imagination" George handed back every lemon that life handed him with an emphatic no and he built his legacy on his own terms.

Day and night, we waste time stuck in limbo from fear, second-guessing, and, most of the time, just being lazy pursuing life from our own preconceived thoughts. In order to change the direction and course of our lives, we must begin with the transformation of the mind and believing in yourself and the god that is inside of you. The moment you realize that you attract into your life whatever your mind is fixated on, your life will never ever be the same again. You will have to work at applying these principles to your ideas and this is not easy. We want to be sure to drive that point home.

Changing the way you think, after thinking a certain way for over twenty or thirty years, will be one of the most difficult challenges you face in your life. However, it must be done if you expect to have the sweeter things in life. Or you could just settle for lemons and make lemonade. However, by nature, we are champions created to rule the earth and everything in it. Like Kings and Queens, those who understand their power, we are to use our minds effectively to thrive and live the life we want to live. "When I released my first album, I honestly had no idea what I was doing, but inside I felt like I had been through the process before. I had to learn to do the track selection, come up with concepts, find feature artist, and market the project. My friends and I put our thinking caps on and got it done. Through our mastermind sessions, we came up with a great plan to promote the project. When we released the project, it received so much buzz that I got an independent record deal a month later. Which I was obliged to take. Prior to this, every negative stone and opinion was thrown my way, but I totally ignored them. I held onto the vision that I had in my mind. All the ideas that I had visualized and stayed focused on, came to fruition because I had a focused desire and a strong belief in myself. This way of thinking should be our intent as we set our minds to do the seemingly impossible. There is a time to be humble and a time to be aggressively centered on getting your goals accomplished, with no apologies.

We are writing this to give you a swift kick in the ass to help you understand the lemons you are accepting are coming to you because you actually did ask for them. If you do not make it clear to your mind how you want your life to be, then your imagination will be on autopilot with no one at the controls. You will have a collage of a life, filled with whatever life hands you, because you are too cowardly to think for yourself and determine what you really want out of life. The only tangible way to remove these lemons from your life is through making better decisions and remaining steadfast on your dreams and intentions in life. The voice that we hear in our head when we talk to ourselves or pray, is in fact the voice of god speaking back to us, giving us an even and direct path to our next step. Do not dismiss this voice as just you answering yourself, but recognize that when you talk to yourself you are in direct communication with god, because the Kingdom is within, not without therefore it begs to reason that a King or Ruler lives within their Kingdom, and the Kingdom is within you, and within you is where you find God, King, Queen, Ruler, Lord of your life.

Our response to that voice can be the determining factor to a positive new journey or missing the mark. By the way, did you realize that missing the mark is sin? Yes, because god is in you and by virtue of creation you are god. Therefore, when you set goals for yourself in life and you do not quite reach them, you feel bad. The reason for this is that you have let yourself down. You missed the mark and now it is time to start over or repent, turn away from that, which caused you to miss the mark, and chart a new course. By doing this, you create a new way of thinking about life and new ways to accomplish your goals.

# 6

# Champions

The Champion is like the grass. The nature of grass is to grow, to flourish, yes; overgrown grassy yards and fields represent prosperity. Cut it down as you may and it will flourish again. This is thought process of winners. These people have an insatiable drive for achievement no matter what happens to them. Against all odds, they have achieved great success. Those counted out by society somehow seem to bounce back stronger than ever just like the grass. These folk are no different from you and me. They are just people who refused to accept no for an answer. They refused to take lemons and make lemonade. So what is it that drives these people? What is their secret? Their secret is really no secret at all. They understand that the word NO was made to be used. When you begin to say no to things in life that you do not want, that is when you begin pushing ahead; the pushing ahead toward what you want, is the handing back of lemons.

For example, a great Champion like Michael Jordan, he knew without a doubt that every night he walked onto the court and the ball hit his hands, the lawn mowers were ready to cut him down. He knew there was going to be a battle every time. Adversaries, foes, and rivals were trying to take the ball away from him to stop him from hitting his goal, literally. You too must understand that as you get involved with the carrying out of your goals, things are going to happen that seem to interfere with what you are trying to accomplish. Knowing this ahead of time and preparing for the distraction in advance will have you moving like a Champion. It is called being proactive, which is the ability to see potential threats and problems before they happen and plan to overcome them. To move forward in the event an issue arises, requires looking at success from all angles. Seeing the worst possible outcome and planning from there. This is not to say you are planning to fail. You plan to win no matter what happens. But if you don't think of potential risks to your ideas and plan a way to keep going forward, then when the shit hits the fan you will be stuck there to smell it.

Part of being proactive is something called visualization. This is what Michael Jordan used during his preparation for games. You could see that there was something behind the eyes of Michael Jordan and that something was VISUALIZATION. It is the ability to see the big picture; you have to play the tape all the way through to the end in your imagination.

Visualization is using the imagination to see every potential threat to your goal and to see how you are going to face this threat, should it appear. Michael Jordan saw himself as capable of making that last second shot under pressure. We mean he literally saw himself in his imagination making the shot before he ever had to make that game winning shot.

Every success and championship that has ever been won or will be had, is done so by visualizing it happening before it ever happens, or as some like to say, believe that ye receive and you shall have whatsoever ye have said. You have to see it in the imagination first. Right here is where you get the power to hand those lemons back, through your imagination. Did you think your imagination was just a way for you to escape reality? No. The imagination is where your reality comes from; the workshop for building the life you want to have. Think about it. Everything around you came from someone's imagination first. The airplane, the automobile, houses, clothes, cell phones, the list goes on and on of things that came from the imagination of people. We think these people are great because of what they have accomplished. Here and now, we tell you they are great because they knew how to use their own minds.

Handing lemons back means that you have a fixed vision in your imagination of what you see and expect. This is a vision of you living the life you truly want to live. When events take place that do not fit into that vision of your future, keep that vision of your future that you believe to be true, ever burning in your imagination. Do not allow distractions to take your mind away from your vision. When you lose sight of your vision, you are in danger of accepting lemons and making lemonade. You stop moving progressively toward your stated goal and you slip back into this mindset of weakness and fear. However, you are a Champion and Champions do not quit. They WIN!

There is a popular recording artist named Jidenna and he has a song called "Chief Don't Run". We have to have that kind of reserve, though my dreams are under attack, I Am the chief of my life and the "Chief Don't Run". Amazingly, there are droves of people who do not know what they want from life and have never imagined more than what they can see. They definitely take whatever life hands them. We implore you now to get yourself some kind of goal and use your imagination to perfect this goal. You will come to find that the more you employ your imagination, the more motivated you become, and the more inspired you will become to act upon your imagination.

Just sitting around daydreaming of better days will not do it. Action is required to move your vision forward. There is no need to know every single step to take before you get started. We live in the 21$^{st}$ century of the information age. Anything and everything you want to know is on YouTube and Google. Therefore, there are no excuses available to claim you do not know how to do this or that. The problem lies in knowing what you want out of life.

People are told to ask god what their purpose is in life, and then told to wait upon the lord for an answer, but let us share another secret with you. The answer to your purpose is given, yes, you do not need to pray or ask anybody about what your purpose is. All you need to do is look in the book of Genesis chapter 1:28, after the creation of man. Over time, these instructions have remained the same. In Genesis, the verse states, "And God blessed them, and God said unto them, be fruitful, and multiply, and replenish the earth, and subdue it: and have dominion over the fish of the sea and over the fowl of the air, and over every living thing that moveth upon the earth".

To be blessed means to have all that you need for fruitfulness. To be fruitful means to be productive or creative, and to multiply means to increase productivity or creativity. This speaks of a powerful person, someone who is in control of his or her now and his or her future. The text in the bible speaks of having absolute rule of the earth and all of the things of the earth. Therefore, it sounds to us that we are supposed to be busy creating, ruling, and taking dominion. But of what, you say? What is it that you are going to create or be productive doing? Well, here is where free will comes in. You have to decide what it is that you like and what you are good at doing. Speaking of which, if you feel you are not good at anything you can always become good at something you choose.

That is another great trait of the mind of a Champion. Champions always prepare and stay prepared by educating themselves on that which interests them. They also practice, practice, practice! "I have a college degree in music theory and composition. To learn to play any instrument and become proficient at it, you have to practice every single day or you will never become proficient". The same is required for any level of success. You have to become educated and learn about things you are interested in so that you can expand that information with experience. Champions do not accept lemons. Michael Jordan understood his purpose and he played through intense physical and psychological pain to gain not one but six Championship rings. This is a great representation of his devotion, commitment, and passion to accomplish his goals.

You must begin each day seeing yourself the way you want to be. Visualizing your life the way you want it to be, not the way it currently is. You have to play a trick on your mind and your five senses in order to get them to believe that what they actually see, feel, taste, hear, and touch is not real, but that only what you say and believe is real. You have to convince those five senses that not what they say is real but what you say is real. Believe me, if you are serious and persistent enough, your five senses will line up with whatever you say. You have to make your mind revert to a childlike imagination when it comes to building your life.

For example, "when my son was 2 years old, he would play with sticks and clothes hangers as if they were airplanes. I must admit, I could see some resemblance of an airplane in the sticks and clothes hangers he chose. I started to tell him one day, "Son, that is not an airplane, but I did not want to interfere with his power to use his imagination. What this did for him was so amazing. His imagination was so vivid that it made me go out and buy him an actual toy plane so he could finally have what he was imagining. He did not know that he had used his mind to make that airplane appear in his reality but I knew". Now you know that if you use your imagination on purpose you can transform your life and create within it, whatever experiences you desire to have. Michael Jordan did it. All Champions do it. Moreover, so can you. Remember that Champions are like grass whose natural tendency is to grow and flourish. Like the grass, cut me down as you may and I will rise and flourish again.

# 7

# Summary

There used to be a television commercial for the United Negro College Fund and the tag line was "A mind is a terrible thing to waste". We did not understand it back then, but we do today. We understand now that when we do not make a decision on what we really want from life, the decision is made for us by default. This is a terrible wasting of the mind. We used to think that reading the bible and only hanging out with people who read the bible was the way to go. However, we soon found ourselves isolated from great people. Therefore, we began to read other books and hang out with people who did not necessarily see things the way we saw them. As a result, we began to grow and advance in life.

We began to meet people whom we never would have met had we stayed boxed inside the "Church Family". We are not knocking the church per se. Most of these non-profit organizations carry out great humanitarian works within the communities they serve. However, If you give yourself an opportunity to meet other people who do not think the way you do, and connect with people who do not look like you, then you might just open the door to your future. We knew a lot of people would say that the characters we mentioned and the television shows are fiction, however, the reason we chose these specific television shows as chapter titles and used theme song ideas as examples is because those shows are a true reflection of life, philosophy, state of mind, and possibility.

Those actors were portraying the real life of someone else in the real world. That is what made these shows attractive during those times. The people in charge of marketing these shows knew who was most likely to watch them. They performed marketing research and understood that the themes would connect with a particular group of people who would relate to the content. This group identifies in whole or in part with one or more of the characters on the television screen, therefore, we used the shows as examples. We know that if you relate to any character on the shows we used, then you will most definitely relate to the information we are sharing about handing lemons back. Life can be tough, but it does not always have to be and it can get to the point where you are enjoying life every day. However, that is up to you.

Neither our book nor its content was written to offend anyone, but rather to incite you to really think about the concepts and philosophies herein presented. Our purpose is to move you to examine your beliefs and be sure that they are your own, and not remnants of someone else's programming. If after you have done a fearless and searching moral inventory, you find that you still believe the same way, then so be it. However, if you find that you are unsure of some of the things that you currently believe, then you know that you have some work in front of you to do.

One of our Mentors, Napoleon Hill, shared a lot of his insight in his classic book, Think and Grow Rich. Neville Goddard, also wrote profoundly about the power of the imagination, and there are many more that have come before us to tell people about the amazing powers we possess as human beings. However, in the beginning, we doubted our mentors and sat on the information for years and then returned to it, as we got older. We understood it better but we still were not quite ready yet. So about thirty years had gone by before we picked up Napoleon Hill's book "Think and Grow Rich" again, and this is when we knew we were ready. We were ready to be open to learning something new and we were ready to accept change. We were ready to hear a different point of view. Even though we initially rejected this philosophy, there was still something deep, deep inside that made us wonder about the validity of this philosophy. That something was the truth from the outside resonating with the truth present inside of us.

That is what led us back with more thirst and desire. The truth was resonating so loudly that we could not rest until we became free in our minds to think thoughts that were congruent with our experiences and not thoughts permeated with the experience of someone else. Some of you who read this book will reject it completely and thus close the door to growth. As one of our mentors put it, you have a very "low teach-ability index". Others will wrestle with the ideas and concepts presented here and yet others will come to understand it quickly. However, understanding it, wrestling with it, and executing it are different worlds. People who obtain information, then go out, and actually act on that information by implementing the things they have learned will most likely achieve their goals.

When you get all the information about something and you, do nothing with it, then you have no one to blame for your circumstances but you. There is absolutely no reason on this earth that you cannot live the life you really desire. You have watched mamma, daddy, grandma, and grandpa all take lemons and make lemonade, but this does not mean that you have to follow their example. This is your generation, if you follow their path, you are destined to end up where they did. I understand that one generation builds upon the next, but if you look down the line at your great grandparents and you see poverty then and you take a look at yourself and see that you were born poor too, then somebody in your family didn't get the memo to build upon the next.

So now you have been officially served the memo and it reads, "You must build the family legacy" whatever that legacy is for you. If great-grandpa or great- grandma were not thinking about you and your future, then you have to become the great-grandpa or great-grandma in the family who thinks about the future of your offspring and prepare a way for them.

If we have not made it clear what we mean by legacy and what we mean by success, let us do so now. We are absolutely talking about financial growth and independence, and yes, we are talking about getting your money game up. We have realized that everything in this life has to do with money. Everybody always wants money for something, and it is apparent we need money for everything. We can't take it with us when we die, but we definitely can't live without it.

Accepting lemons and making lemonade is about being broke and choosing to stay broke mentally, financially, socially, spiritually, and in any other way imaginable. If you doubt that everything is about money then let us know if you think the pastor is going to keep showing up to preach when the collection plate does not support their lifestyle. Some pastors actually work outside their ministry and therefore do not burden their parishioners. We are not talking about them. Better yet, let us see if you keep showing up at your place of employment without getting a paycheck. When that money situation changes or dries up, you are out of there. The reason is that you need money. So let us stop pretending that we are okay with minimum wage, or low paying jobs, and do something about it. People who work for minimum wage have minimum skills most of the time, so if you want better wages you have to improve your skills. If you do not improve your skills then you are accepting lemons and making lemonade. We think it is fair to drive home the point that needing money is right up there with needing air, and only those who have no money are telling you that you should not make money so important.

Well, you can follow that crowd if you like, but as for us, we must set a firm financial foundation so our families can have more options in life. We understand, everybody does not want to be rich, but, nobody wants to be poor either. So it is either the haves or the have-not's, there really is no middle ground. Which one are you? We are in the haves lane. Having money and things, helps to occupy and feed the imagination. Even more, we are able to be more creative when we have more to work with. The imagination is designed to help us acquire more things to work with so that we can imagine even more possibilities.

We can hear the quote now, "Money is the root of all evil". To be clear it actually says that the "Love of money is the root of all evil". So we are not talking about loving money here, we are talking about the absolute need for money, and the love of having it. Life is designed to function well with money and not so well without it. Jesus understood money clearly, during tax season in the bible. There is a story about Jesus, who sent one of his disciples down to the water and told him there would be a fish there. Jesus told him that he should take up the fish and open its mouth and there you will find gold coins. The disciple was instructed to take the coins and pay the taxes.

Jesus understood, that in order to continue to function in this society he needed money. Without those taxes paid, they would have shut their program down. You must stop taking lemons and making lemonade. Get yourself a business and learn how to build something for yourself and your family. I mean wouldn't it be nice to know that when your grand kids grow up they will already have a platform from which to launch their dreams? A platform established by you, not just about money, but also resources and rich relationships.

If you do this right and really work at it, your family will never have to worry about how their bills will be paid. You have to set the family business in motion so that they will always have access to making money and nobody can ever close the door in their face.

# 8

# About the Authors

## Donald Rose

Donald Rose is a native of Houston Texas, born and raised in Kashmere Gardens, the northeast district of Houston. It was a tough neighborhood to grow up in. Seeing prostitutes, hustlers, addicts, and peddlers on the block was an ordinary day. He was raised by his grandparents, and they did their best to shelter him from the ills of the streets, to provide stability in his life. He was reared in a strict, religious home where, on the weekends, the Sabbath which began and ended on (Friday sunset to Saturday sunset) was top priority. At the Rose' residence, on the Sabbath, there was no watching television; church music filled the air, and spending the majority of Saturday at church was the normal agenda. Within the confines of his sheltering is where Donald first learned how to use his imagination to create.

His gifts and talents were cultivated at a young age. He got his start acting in plays, singing in the school and church choir, and playing sports. One gift he seemed to master early on was writing and creating music. Eventually his love for writing took him on a journey from recording demo tapes in his bedroom to becoming a respected underground hip-hop artist in his city. He attributes his growth as a writer and musician to learning how to use his thoughts to paint pictures with words, and literally make something from nothing. These tools played a huge part in his unwavering focus. This same focus, however, would be tested when he was diagnosed with a chronic illness.

"I remember life taking a drastic turn for me in June of 1987, during the summer. After returning home from a family trip to Mexico, I fell very ill. This, I can honestly say, was the worst week I have ever experienced through this electric journey of life. My appetite was nonexistent. I was sleeping all day and night. My energy was on such a low vibration it made it difficult to do anything physical like walk. During this time, I lost around 30 thirty pounds and for the life of me, I could not stop urinating. I was drastically sluggish and felt like I was in a blurred dream. My grandmother and mother were my angels. When they saw that I was not getting any better, I was rushed to the emergency room where I was later diagnosed with Type 1 Diabetes (also known as juvenile diabetes).

"The doctor stated it was hereditary and it wasn't due to my diet or anything. It was weird how my body was good and functioning one day and all of a sudden it felt like my body was attacking itself. In the blink of an eye, my whole world was changed forever. Life was trying to hand me a GIGANTIC tree of lemons. Being an 11-year-old African American male with this new "condition", another reconditioning and transformation of the mind had to place. Since I was a young child, I've always been a team player and down to make what seems impossible, possible. So it wasn't really that hard of a transition. But, what I did have to get used to was the insulin injections everyday. Once the doctors, nurses, and my family explained that without taking this medicine I run the risk having life threatening complications, it was a no-brainer.

Interestingly, as I was getting adjusted to this new consciousness of living, people would continue trying to hand me lemons with comments of fear and restrictions of what they thought diabetes would or could do to me. It's moments like this where my reaction to everybody's opinion of their own insecurities could have been harmful to me, if I chose to believe their opinions and dwell in them."

As an indigo child, Donald chose to walk his path on his terms with no fear and to live a healthy, confident life to the fullest. Unexpected curve balls were thrown his way as an adult, which would test his faith. From his first marriage failing, losing most of his possessions due to financial problems, and having to start over from square one. Through the power of creating his reality with his imagination and beliefs, he turned his life around with super high vibrations. He is involved in some very profitable ventures from films & investing to publishing and real estate. He is one-half of The Write Brothers of The Write Society. He gives credit to his new balance, success, and the drive to achieve more and be more from the support and connection with his wife, Neitra.

Donald attended and graduated from Sam Houston State University with a Bachelors Degree in Business Administration. He has volunteered and dedicated his time in the non-profit sector working as an advocate for youth and the homeless. He is well known in the media, music, and acting community in Houston Texas. You can hear him on the podcast "From Houston, With Love" on allrealradio.com. He is also the founder of the media and film company Talented Media Group.

Writing, music, and film are a healthy medium that has allowed Donald to create his reality, one project at a time. Either the projects he has created or collaborated on, always has a message with a relevant theme attached. The stories, songs, and short films he has created, have helped him to transfer the electrifying energy he's had since youth growing up in Fifth Ward. He submits this book as evidence of the power of the imagination.

**Randy Hannah**

Randy Hannah was born in 1976, when the peace and love era was wrapping up to make way for the crack epidemic. His future was uncertain, and poverty was the lay of the land. He was raised on the South side of Houston Texas, in a neighborhood named South Park in the 1980's. It was a place where knowing how to fight was a necessity if you wanted to come outside and play in the streets with everyone else otherwise you stayed on the porch and watched the other kids laugh and play. His upbringing was rigorously religious, raised as a Seventh Day Adventist he was a bit of a square in comparison to those he was growing up with in

South Park. He spoke a little more proper than most of his peers and he dressed quite differently from the rest too. It would be normal to see him walking to school in a three-piece suite on a Tuesday morning in High school in the 90's.

On Friday nights instead of a sleep over at a friend's house, he would be in the living room with his two sisters and his grandmother singing hymns and receiving instruction from the bible, on Saturday morning while his friends slept in late, and lounged around watching cartoons, Randy was getting dressed for church and the only thing playing was gospel music. This was his life until the age of 15, when he began to realize that not only was he different from his peers, he was different from the people who were giving him religious instruction too.

He thought about the sermons and the cliches the pastor would use, and then he'd go back home and read the scripture and compare what the preacher said to what was written and it often didn't add up. This was unsettling to Randy. He could not shake this nagging desire for more information so he sought out more on life in general, he began to read other books that had to do with self and the improvement of self, and so the journey began. To make a long story short, this guy made some very stupid and poor choices with his life early on, and when you put young, stupid, and poor together you get a ruined life by age 21. After he lost his record deal with Rap-a-Lot Records in 1997, he tried to sell crack cocaine and found out quickly that he wasn't cut out to be a drug dealer. So he was stuck with a fifty dollar pack of crack and and ounce of marijuana on his 21st birthday. Deeply depressed, he began to relieve the pain of loosing his record deal and all of the other pains from a broken home by mixing crack and weed, what's called a Primo or a Mackball, and smoking it. Soon he became a full blown crack addict. He got into more legal trouble and ultimately ended up in prison for 3 years. It was there in the belly of the beast at age 27 that Randy Hannah became a man and matured.

Surrounded by violence daily in prison he tuned it out by reading books on self-improvement and entrepreneurship. He had nothing else to do but read, and he literally read all-day and late into the night for three years straight. However, this still was not enough. He needed more and he found it, in prison, when he enrolled in a class called Cognitive Intervention. At first, this was just a way to get away from the cell block. Nevertheless every day, Mr. Munson the instructor, would hand out a newspaper, pick an article, and everyone would read it. After reading it, Mr. Munson would say: "So what cha think"? He did not care what you thought he just wanted you to actively think. This method repeated day in and day out for 6 months straight was a tool designed to develop critical thinking skills. Randy had never paid attention to his thoughts or his thought process. This class exposed his thinking or lack thereof and he was astonished to find out that, his thoughts were very poor and his thoughts are what landed him in prison. He was released from prison in 2006 and reunited with his wife Rhonda who stood by him the whole time and made sure he had a stable foundation to come home to.

As he began his new journey, he relocated his family to St. Louis Missouri in 2010, attended and graduated college in with a degree in music theory and composition. He was inducted into Phi Theta Kappa the largest International Honor Society among two-year colleges and he served as Chapter President of Xi Epsilon, Saint Louis Community College at Forest Park. Graduating with honors, he received several scholarships and leadership awards for his service to the community and was elected Vice President of Student Government and served as a mentor for the African American Male Initiative.

He went on to attend the Pierre Laclede Honors College at the University of Missouri Saint Louis Majoring in Liberal Arts. His focus and determination to live and help other people understand that the power of thought has miraculous qualities is evident in the life he now enjoys with his family as a happy peaceful man. It is also evidenced in the material covered in this book through his literary contribution. There is so much more to his story but it is beyond the scope of this book, therefore we submit a small sample of the road traveled by one of the Write Bothers. Randy Hannah learned from childhood to pick up a pen or pencil and write to express his feelings and thoughts through the creation of music, songs, and poems. He has continued his love of writing about life and his experiences. Therefore he submits this book as evidence of the power of the mind and the power of self.

www.ingramcontent.com/pod-product-compliance
Lightning Source LLC
Chambersburg PA
CBHW020023050426
42450CB00005B/617